NF419955

I wish to dedicate this book to all the people who have been wondering what to do and how to do it for all their lives. This book is an example of how you can get rid of the "head trash" and live the life you always have seen other people live.

To Mark Robert Deaver: You have been there through most of my adult life, seeing what accomplishments I attained, and also wondering what I was thinking when things did go bad. I wouldn't trade it for the world.

To Jason Grossman (The Angry Australian) Being a part of your coaching group is the most eye-opening experience of my life. Telling me to write a book was the meanest thing anyone has had me do, yet you encouraged me to get it started, and here it is. This would never have happened without your guidance (well, growling!)

To John Robertson, DTM: When you took me on as a mentee, I had no idea what to expect. 5 months later, I am the president of the charter group Writer's Ink Toastmasters. None of this would have happened without your guidance and confidence. Thank you

To Heather Seal: Part of this is your fault! Without you standing outside the Toastmasters after meeting at the meeting place, almost stomping your foot and telling me to publish this for sale, this wouldn't have happened. Thank you for giving me that push to get this done!

Vincent Amado: Where would I be without you? You have kept me organized, worked on all of my social media, and helped get the word out about how and who I wanted to help. Without you, I wouldn't be anywhere close to where I am today! Thank you!

Contents:

Prologue

Imagine what you will do tomorrow. What does that look like? Waking up, doing the usual morning ritual, and going to work. That's how it usually works. That's what we do every day. So what's to be done when it comes to getting out of that rut?

First, what is your mindset? What are you anticipating? Another day at work, dealing with the same predictable and anticipated problems and events?

Or are you really ready to make a change? Taking that first step, making that decision to change the outcome of the day? This is known as the **"I'VE HAD IT!"** moment. This is where true change starts. This is where you make the decision to change the outcome of your future.

When you wake up tomorrow, there is something I want you to tell yourself. Say the following words out loud, then see how you feel. "Today is going to be better than yesterday." It might take a minute, but you will feel a bit better about the day.

This is the first step in ending self-doubt in your daily life. The more you are confident, the more you will want to do. When you want to do more, you will have a better overall outlook on your day, and your life.

People talk a lot about what they want out of life. But very few take the time and take the steps needed to accomplish their goals. Why is that? Self-doubt shrinks their ambitions. Their circle of happiness gets smaller and smaller to the point where what they are doing now makes them content. But are they actually content, or are they just avoiding both the fear of failure and even worse, the fear of success? Something to think about.

There are other sources of finding motivation in your life. One is who you associate with. There is a very big commonality between who you associate with and your outlook on life. If the people you hang out with are continually blaming everyone else for their situation, this might be an indication of where the root of the problem is. We are the product of the 5 people we associate with most often. Now think about that. Think about the 5 people you associate with on a regular basis. What are they saying? What are they doing on a daily basis? This is a huge indicator of not only what they are doing, but also what you are thinking.

If you control your thoughts, this also controls your actions, thus controlling your outlook on life, and in turn both the fear of failure and the fear of success.

A MEMORY COMES TO MIND. Something that has stuck in my mind for the past 5 years. I was in the oilfield, and I had made great friends with the head of maintenance there. We would hang out and think of ways to have the oilfield make us more money than we were making (don't get me wrong, we were making **BANK** at the time, we just were thinking about how to make more). We would always help each other out no matter what the issue was or what was going on.

One time I was in the yard and it was about an hour or so before log out time. Here he comes, and he is holding a piece of paper in his hand. He asks me "hey, could you be a fire watch for a quick welding job?" I said of course, what is the project? He told me "I am welding mounting plates for the new reel air hoses for the winch trucks". Ok so we go into the shop, I clear out all of the flammable materials in the immediate vicinity, and we get started. I found myself watching him and wishing I asked him if

I could give it a try. I did have a bit of teaching on welding, and it seemed easy enough.

After he was done, I told him what I was thinking. He looked me dead in the eyes with a hurt expression. "All you had to do was ask" was what he said. The reason for the hurt expression was because this was the last plate that had to be welded. There were no more chances to do it. And I could tell this was a man who loved teaching others his craft. I told him I wasn't afraid you would have said no, I was afraid you would say yes.

See how the fear of success can hinder your growth? I wasn't afraid of failure. I knew he would stop me if I was getting into a bad situation. And I knew I wouldn't take offense at him giving instruction. All he would be wanting to do was make me a better welder.

And this, ladies and gentlemen, is an example of how the fear of not succeeding in something, but also how the fear of failure can hinder just about everything you want to accomplish in life or career.

So get out of your own head, don't be afraid to fail, and get ready to excel at anything you want to accomplish!

6

Chapter 1:

Introduction

From an early age, my life was devoid of most luxuries and opportunities that most children enjoy. Growing up in rural Oklahoma, success seemed like an elusive dream. Very limited resources were available for personal development and growth.

One of my earliest memories dates back to when I was about two years old. I was in one of those little pedal powered cars, gleefully navigating its pedals, until I made an impulsive decision to venture off the front porch, leaving my parents in a state of panicked surprise. Looking back, that moment stands out as the first vivid memory etched into my mind.

My parents belonged to the hardworking class, with my father being a mechanic who had recently returned from serving in the Vietnam War. However, when the government introduced stricter emission controls on vehicles, he decided to seek alternative employment., Meanwhile my mother dedicated herself to being a stay-at-home mom, caring for me during my early years. Our modest lives were further complicated by the rural setting of our community, where opportunities for advancement were scarce.

Within my family, a pervasive victim mentality and an attitude of achieving more with less were prevalent. These mindsets often dominated our conversations around the dinner table, shaping my early beliefs and understanding of the world.

Eventually, my father managed to transition away from being a mechanic by joining the Operating Engineers union. Basically being a crane operator, he was part of construction crews in the Oklahoma City area building the taller buildings and other plants such as the GM manufacturing plant in eastern Oklahoma City.

However, my mother's health began to deteriorate. She was starting to experience sight loss and developing Multiple Sclerosis which ultimately led to her being classified as disabled.

It was during this time, around 2 weeks from Thanksgiving in 1982, that my father abruptly left. I recall standing in the living room, witnessing a heated discussion, then his subsequent departure, leaving myself and my mom in tears. I am pretty sure this was the gateway for her spiral towards a victim mentality, with the phrase "I am always wrong" being used a lot when something didn't work out. As for me, at about 10 years of age, I was primarily focused on learning and exploring the world, oblivious to the lasting impact these circumstances would have on my perception of how things should work in the world.

To fill the void left by my father's absence, my step-grandfather stood in. However, having never raised children of his own and growing up during the Dust Bowl and the Great Depression, he struggled to navigate the complexities of parenting a confused and self-esteem-depleted child like myself. Sadly, he resorted to employing the same methods of discipline and survival that his own father had imposed during the time he grew up. While I won't go into detail about specifics, it is important to acknowledge the immense pain that characterized this period of my life.

As I matured, I gradually realized there were alternative ways to live and perceive the world. Observing other children at school and catching glimpses of opportunities during occasional weekend trips to the grocery store opened my eyes to the possibilities beyond my limited beliefs and learned behaviors. However, the barriers of self-confidence, motivation, and self-esteem that had taken root within me hindered my ability to recognize and seize these opportunities. The continuous cycle of blame, the lack of self-assurance, and the distressing experience of being bullied further contributed to my dread of attending school.

After enduring these circumstances for a prolonged period of five years, my father unexpectedly reached out and offered the chance to live with him. He was in a big city, no one knows who I am, so there isn't a reason to be bullied. This sounded like paradise! In leaving behind the abuse inflicted by my step-grandfather and the torment of school, it appeared as a fresh start. aYet, the scars and deeply ingrained patterns had already taken hold, influencing my perceptions and reactions as I transitioned to this new environment.

However, trust proved to be elusive, and seeing genuine support from manipulative mind games became a daunting task due to my inherent mistrust of others.This lack of mistrust further complicated my personal growth, making it challenging to fully embrace positive experiences and relationships.

In my father's new life, marked by his remarriage, I found myself feeling like an outsider. Despite occasional displays of support, hurtful phrases from my step-mother, such as "I hate people like you", served to reinforce my sense of alienation.

Additionally, my father's demanding job as a truck driver often kept him away for extended periods, leaving limited opportunities for quality family time.

The combination of these early experiences, ranging from abuse and bullying to strained relationships and limited opportunities, left an indelible mark on my worldview. They shaped my thoughts, beliefs, and perspectives regarding myself and the world around me.

In the forthcoming chapters, I will take you on a transformation journey, sharing the five core pillars of the foundation of change I developed through my own life experiences. These core parts of the foundation serve as the bedrock of my life coaching program, empowering others to unlock their fullest potential.

Chapter 2:
The Five Core Foundations Of Transformation

In this chapter, we will explore the five parts of the foundation that empower you to transform your life. These cores serve as the foundation for breaking free from limiting thoughts, unlocking your potential, and creating the life you desire. Let's dive into each pillar and discover how they reshape your perspective, guiding you towards a more fulfilling and purposeful life.

SELF-CONFIDENCE

The journey begins by recognizing and challenging your limiting thoughts. What's been holding you back? It's time to break free from the mindset that change is impossible. It's time to take out the "head trash"- all those thoughts and beliefs that have been holding you back from getting what you want out of life. Self-Confidence is the key-it empowers you to believe in your abilities and embrace the learning curve that comes with growth.

12

Here's what you can do:

- Identify your strengths and talents

- Surround yourself with positive relationships that support and uplift you

- Embrace mistakes and learn from them

- Set healthy boundaries and assert yourself

- Embrace challenges that push you out of your comfort zone.

Remember, self-confidence isn't about instant success but about knowing that you will get it figured out, all you have to do is keep working at it.

SELF-MOTIVATION

With our building self-confidence, we ignite self-motivation-the driving force behind taking action. Even small actions, like making your bed in the morning, can have a great impact on your day. Let's explore the four elements of self-motivation:

- Personal drive to achieve: Tap into your competitive spirit and inner desire for growth.

- Commitment to personal goal: Stay dedicated to your aspirations, even in the face of distractions. Patience and persistence will lead you to success.

- Initiative: taking charge of your life by proactively tackling tasks, thinking ahead, and going the extra mile.

- Optimism: Cultivate a positive outlook that fuels your motivation and instills confidence in your ability to overcome challenges.

Optimism is particularly important. Believe in your ability to accomplish tasks and trust that you can find the right path to reach your goals. Embrace optimism as the driving force behind your actions.

SELF-ESTEEM

Self-esteem plays a vital role in your journey and success. Release the grip of self-loathing, lack of motivation, and feeling inadequate. Embrace the fact that you are worthy of great things and capable of achieving what you set out to accomplish.

This is also a transitional step. While we have been building our confidence and motivation, our self-esteem has also been building. All that is needed now is to both reflect on what we have accomplished to this point and prepare for what is coming next.

Right now, we can boost self-esteem with these steps:

- Remind yourself of your inherent worthiness

- Believe in your ability to accomplish your goals and tasks

- Let go of concerns about others' opinions and focus on your own happiness. Remember, your perception of yourself holds immense power. Embrace a positive self-image and let go of self-doubt.

RELATIONSHIPS

Healthy relationships are essential for a fulfilling life. Consider the impact of the people you surround yourself with, both personally and professionally. Negative relationships can drain your energy and hinder your progress, while positive relationships can support and uplift you. Reflect on the following:

- Evaluate your relationships and identify those that bring negativity into your life.

- Prioritize healthy relationships that contribute positively to your well-being.

- Realize that maintaining boundaries becomes easier with great relationships in your life.

These points will be telling when it comes to who is actually with you or trying to pull you down. Esteem not only comes from within, but it is hugely affected by people around you as well.

CAREER:

Your career significantly impacts your overall well-being and life satisfaction. Assess your level of fulfillment in your current work. Do you feel energized and fulfilled, or do you dread going to work? Evaluating your career path is crucial to maintaining progress in the previous cores. Consider the following:

- Do you genuinely enjoy your work, or is it time for a change?
- Does your work leave you feeling energized and satisfied?
- Are there growth opportunities and challenges in your current career?

Answering these questions honestly will guide you towards making necessary changes in your career to align it with your personal growth and fulfillment.

BRINGING IT ALL TOGETHER

By addressing these five cores-limiting thoughts, self-confidence, self-motivation, self-esteem, relationships, and career-you can embark on a transformative journey towards a more fulfilling life. Life is short, and there is no need to waste it with negative thoughts.

As you progressively build your foundation, you will unlock your true potential and create the life you were meant to live. Embrace the power within you to break free from self-imposed limitations, cultivate positive relationships, and pursue a career that brings you joy. Stay committed to your growth, and step by step, you'll realize the absolutely great life you deserve.

Conclusion

Congratulations on completing this chapter and gaining insights into the five cores of your self-foundation. Each core serves as a strong foundation for persona; growth, guiding you towards a life filled with confidence, motivation, self-esteem, fulfilling relationships, and a satisfying career. Embracing these cores and taking action will bring about remarkable changes as you unleash your true potential.

Remember, your journey towards self-confidence and personal transformation is unique to you. Be patient with yourself, celebrate your progress, and always remember that you have the power to create the life you want. In the upcoming chapters, we will dive deep into each core, exploring strategies and techniques that will propel you forward on your path of personal growth.

So buckle up! Get ready for a ride! Together, we will explore the depths of each core and equip you with the tools and insights you need to thrive. Let's get this journey of self-discovery and empowerment started!

Chapter 3:

Self-Confidence

Doing the same thing over and over again expecting a different result is the truest form of insanity-
Albert Einstein

INTRODUCTION:

In this chapter, we will explore the transformative power of self-confidence. It's a quality that many of us desire but often struggle with. The journey toward self-confidence is often filled with fear, self-doubt, and negative thoughts that hold us back from attaining our true potential. However, through personal experiences and the lessons I've learned, I discovered that self-confidence is not an elusive trait reserved for a select few. It is a skill that can be developed and maintained with dedication and the right mindset.

THE IMPRISONMENT OF Negative Thoughts:

There was a time when I felt trapped by fear and self-doubt. A vivid memory stands out to me: myself and my step-grandfather were putting skirting around a mobile home he had purchased. This was to protect the plumbing from freezing in the winter. As I helped, he would break drill bit after drill bit while drilling the screw holes for the screws that were to hold everything together. I was under the house holding my foot against where he was drilling. So naturally he would blame me every time the bit broke. No matter what actually happened, I was blamed. The constant beatings and yelling reinforced the belief that I was not good enough to do what was needed. These experiences took their toll on me in my confidence and question if I was even worthy of being alive. It felt like I was wearing an open parachute and walking into a headwind. No matter what anyone else told me or showed me, There was the prevailing thought of unworthiness. But even then, in the depths of self-doubt and esteem, I realized I didn't want to just exist-I wanted to live!

FREEING MYSELF FROM My Own Prison:

One day, in my late 30's a realization hit me like lightning: I was imprisoning myself! The prison was constructed by negative thoughts, belief that I wasn't good at anything, and not worthy of respect. And it was up to me to unlock the doors keeping me in this mindset. I had the power and authority to free myself from this self-imposed prison. I also had the power to embrace myself and my accomplishments, my beliefs, and my aspirations.

Let's do a comparison: If we are the warden of our prison, just as someone else is a warden of a prison, what does the warden carry with them? KEYS! That's what a warden carries! The warden has the ability to open any door, unlock any lock, and let anyone free. This especially applies to you! Since you are not regulated by anyone other than yourself, you have the power AND authority to unlock those doors, walk through it, and take the first step in your new path!

Starting The Climb:

To begin my journey toward self-confidence, I had to stop digging. I realized that doing the same thing over and over, expecting different results, was a recipe for disaster. The feeling of hopelessness and depression were consuming me, leaving me with a sense of complete failure. That moment became my turning point-I declared "I'VE HAD IT! I'M NOT DOING THIS ANYMORE!" It was the moment of clarity that led to the realization change was necessary.

A Pivotal Memory:

During this process, a particular memory resurfaced-one that reminded me of a crucial turning point in my journey towards self-confidence. It was a memory of my step-grandfather, a skilled welder who had set out to teach me his craft. However, his teaching style resembled that of a drill instructor. As a 12-year-old with pre-existing self-confidence issues, his approach didn't sit well with me. At that moment, I did what any kid would do: I followed the instructions to the best of my ability, got out of there, and ran back to my house, where I hid for the rest of the day.

The Weight of Self-Doubt

Following that incident, the weight of self-doubt settled in. I sought solace in hiding, hoping to avoid any future instances that might bring disappointment to my step-grandfather and, more importantly, to myself. It became a coping mechanism-a way to shield myself from discomfort and the fear of not meeting expectations.

CONFRONTING CHALLENGES and Overcoming Obstacles:

This memory serves as a reminder of the challenges I faced on my path to self-confidence. It highlights the significant impact of external influences, such as a harsh teaching style, can have on an individual's self-perception. However, it also underscores the importance of resilience and the need to confront and overcome these obstacles. True self-confidence isn't built on avoiding challenges but facing them head-on and learning from the experiences. It also doesn't mean you know everything about a certain topic. It DOES mean you can figure it out, and that is more important than knowing everything going in.

UNRAVELING THE KEYS to Self-Confidence

So, how do we gain self-confidence? Let's explore some practical strategies and insights:

1. Practice Self-Care: Prioritize taking care of yourself physically, mentally, and emotionally. Get enough sleep, eat healthy, and engage in activities that bring you joy and relaxation.

2. Set Achievable Goals: Start with small, attainable goals and <u>celebrate</u> those accomplishments along the way. Gradually work your way up to bigger goals, building confidence along the way with each achievement.

3. Focus On Your Strengths: Instead of comparing yourself to others or dwelling on your weaknesses, shift your focus to your strengths. Identify your unique talents and abilities and build on them.

4. Surround Yourself With Positive Influences: Surround yourself with people who support and encourage you. Limit your time and energy with individuals who bring you down or make you feel bad about yourself or others. Seek out positive relationships that uplift and inspire you.

5. Challenge Negative Thoughts: When negative thoughts arise, challenge them! Ask yourself "What's the problem?" "Where is this coming from?" Replace

them with positive, self-affirming thoughts. Practice self-compassion and remind yourself of your worth.

6. Embrace Failure and Learn From Mistakes: Recognize that failure is a part of the learning process. Learn from your mistakes and view them as opportunities for growth. Build a growth mindset that sees setbacks as stepping stones to success.

7. Be Assertive and Set Boundaries: Take control of your life by learning to be assertive. Express your needs, desires, and opinions confidently and respectfully. Set boundaries to protect your well-being and prioritize your own values.

8. Step Out of Your Comfort Zone: Give yourself challenges by trying new things. Step out of your comfort regularly, regardless of how big or small the change might be. Embrace the unknown and embrace personal growth.

9. Recognize Your Talents and Skills: Take the time to recognize your abilities and acknowledge what you are good at. Celebrate your strengths and talents and use them as a foundation for building self-confidence.

10. Embrace Self-Kindness: Be kind to yourself, especially during moments of doubt or perceived failure. Treat yourself with compassion and understanding just as you would a close friend.

Building self-confidence is a marathon, not a sprint. It is a continuous journey of self-discovery, growth, and resilience. By starting self-care habits, setting achievable goals, focusing on strengths, surrounding yourself with positive influences, challenging negative thoughts, and embracing failure as a learning opportunity, you will unlock the doors to self-confidence. Remember, it takes time and effort, but with practice and determination, it is achievable. Embrace the journey, learn from every part of it, and believe in your own potential.

Buckle up, buttercup! This journey to self-confidence will be filled with ups and downs, but I promise you, it will be worth it! Embrace the challenges, confront your fears, and celebrate your progress. Self-confidence is within reach-grab onto it and unleash your true potential!

Chapter 4:
Self-Motivation

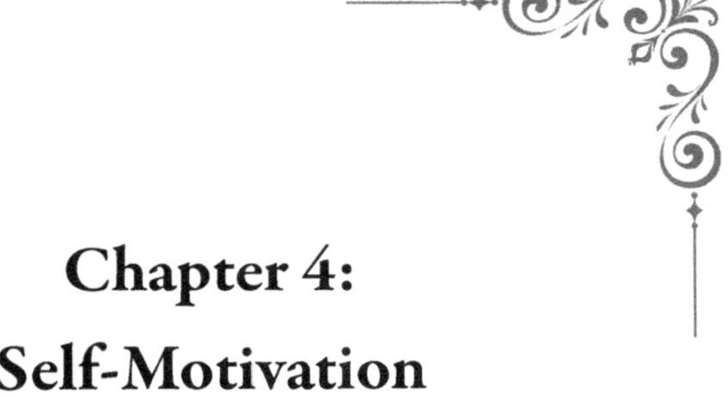

"Stay away from those people who try to disparage your ambitions. Small minds will always do that, but great minds will give you a feeling that you can become great too." — Mark Twain

Introduction:

Self-Motivation is the driving force behind success. It is the energy and determination that comes from within, propelling us to pursue our goals and take action towards our desired outcomes. Without self-motivation, even the most confident and talented people in the world can struggle to achieve their aspirations. In this chapter, we will explore the power of self-motivation and discover practical strategies to cultivate it in our lives.

The Imprisonment of Negative Influences

During my youth, I faced discouragement and negative influences that hindered my self-motivation. People around me would tell me what I couldn't do, paralyzing my belief in my own abilities. One incident that stands out is when I wanted to ride my bicycle to the high school pool, a distance of 5 miles. Mind you, I wasn't 7 or 8, but 13, and during the summers I would ride that thing for most of the day. So despite these facts, no one let me go. I was convinced by my step-grandfather I was incapable of doing it. This experience, among a host of others, reinforced the belief that I couldn't achieve any goal I set out to do, thus limiting my motivation and shooting down any confidence I had.

SETTING MEANINGFUL and Realistic Goals

So to build self-motivation, it is essential to set meaningful and realistic goals. Without clear objectives, it becomes difficult to stay motivated and focused. However, it is equally important to ensure that our goals are attainable and within easy reach. For example, you probably can't hop into a NASCAR and win the Daytona 500, but you can buy a ticket and watch it! You can also go to a training facility and learn how to race, then enter the 500. That's just an example of setting goals, then taking the steps to achieve that goal.

I recall an incident where I attempted to remove an engine from my first car. It threw a lifter, so the whole engine had to be replaced. I didn't have a shop to lift the engine out all at once, but I knew if I took it out part by part, I could get it done, thus not needing to take the whole car to a shop and having to pay more for removing the engine.

Well here comes dad, telling me I couldn't do it, and I was wasting my time even attempting. He stated we need to get the oil out of the engine, then he will put it on the car hauler he was driving at the time, then we will take it to a shop he knew of. Well, since I already had the heads and the oil pan off the engine, this was already accomplished. The car was never put on the hauler, and thus the car never got fixed. This lack of support and belief in my abilities destroyed my motivation, thus destroying my confidence. Even with a plan, and a good plan, people and instances can come in and disrupt your motivation, then your confidence.

Breaking Down Goals into Manageable Steps:

To prevent feelings of being overwhelmed and intimidated, breaking down our goals into smaller, manageable steps is important. Rather than attempting to tackle the entire goal at once, we can divide it into smaller tasks. For instance, if our goal is to write a book, we can start with brainstorming ideas, creating an outline, writing one chapter at a time, editing and revising, then finally publishing the book. By focusing on one step at a time, we can maintain our motivation and make consistent progress.

Accountability and Overcoming Obstacles

Accountability plays a very important role in self-motivation. Tracking our progress and holding ourselves accountable helps us stay on track and maintain our motivation. In my own journey, distractions and a lack of understanding from others often disrupted my focus and commitment. Additionally, I didn't have the opportunity to seek support and guidance from others due to various limitations. Overcoming obstacles and maintaining self-motivation require strategies such as practicing self-compassion, visualizing success, celebrating accomplishments, and surrounding ourselves with positivity.

EMBRACING THE SELF-Motivation Journey:

Cultivating self-motivation is a journey that requires patience, perseverance, and self-reflection. Here are additional practical tips to enhance your self-motivation:

1) Find Your Why: Discover your underlying motivations and connect with the deeper reasons behind your goals. Understanding why you want to achieve something can ignite a strong sense of self-motivation

2) Create A Vision Board: Visualize your desired outcomes by creating a vision board. Gather images, quotes, and affirmations that represent your goals and display them in a prominent place as a daily reminder of what you're working towards.

3) Practice Positive Self-Talk: Replace self-doubt and negative self-talk with positive affirmations and empowering thoughts. Speak to yourself kindly and believe in your capabilities. Remember, we are the hardest on ourselves than anyone else on the planet.

4) Seek Inspiration: Surround yourself with sources of inspiration that align with your goals. Read books, listen to podcasts, and engage with individuals who have achieved what you desire. Their success stories can fuel your motivation.

5) Stay Flexible: Adapt to unexpected challenges and changes in your journey. Embrace a flexible mindset that allows you to adjust your plans while staying

focused on your ultimate goal.

6) Celebrate Milestones: Recognize and celebrate each milestone you achieve along the way. Acknowledge your progress and reward yourself and dedication you've put into reaching each milestone.

7) Find an Accountability Partner: Share your goals and progress with someone you trust. Having an accountability partner can provide support, encouragement, and a sense of shared responsibility to stay motivated.

Conclusion:

Self-Motivation is a vital support of success. By understanding what motivates us, setting meaningful and realistic goals, breaking them down into manageable steps, and holding ourselves accountable, we can cultivate self-motivation in our lives. Despite obstacles and setbacks, we must not let them derail our progress. By practicing self-compassion, visualizing success, celebrating achievements, and embracing additional strategies like finding our "why", creating a vision board, practicing positive self-talk, seeking inspiration, staying flexible, celebrating milestones, and finding an accountability partner, we can improve our self-motivation and propel ourselves towards achieving our goals. Remember, your self-motivation is within your control. Harness it, and watch as you accomplish your goals and aspirations!

Chapter 5:
Reclaiming Your Worth:
Building Your Self-Esteem

"One's dignity may be assaulted, vandalized, and cruelly mocked,
but it can never be taken away unless it is surrendered"
Michael J. Fox

I remember back to when I was about 13. I was outside with my step-grandfather, discussing how we would approach a task. It was a summer day, and as is typical with summer bugs were bussing around. That's what they do, I'm sure it's in their contract.

Anyway, there was this one (probably just gotten his wings) and it's a safe bet he was having trouble controlling his flight. And he flew right into my nose. Right on the tip of my nose. Now anyone who gets touched unexpectedly there will flinch. I'm not talking about getting hit, just an unexpected touch.

Of course I flinched. The next thing I know, this ham-sized fist crashed into the side of my face, accompanied by a furious outpouring of anger about not my not paying attention and a lack of respect. I managed to interject, explaining that I had merely been bumped by a bug. Yet, my explanation fell on deaf ears and the rant continued, berating me for not paying attention to his words.

At that moment, standing up for myself seemed impossible. The threat of more blows left me paralyzed, and thus continued the unraveling of my self-esteem. Unable to assert the truth and silenced by the unwarranted tirade about attentiveness, my self-worth crumbled.

Throughout my adulthood, this lack of self-esteem haunted me. Believing I was unworthy of being heard, I bottled up my emotions until the pressure became too great, resulting in explosive outbursts, just like he would do (yet another learned behavior). It became clear that I had learned a damaging pattern, one that needed to be broken.

If we go back through our experiences, we can point to any number of instances where our fear of success hindered our progress in life. These instances are a result of a lack of self-esteem.

I recall a particular time where I was working in the oilfield. I was on winch truck duty, waiting to be dispatched on some sort of equipment move. It was close to the end of my shift, so it was pretty clear I wasn't going out. Here comes the mechanic on duty. He and I were pretty good friends, so we hung out a lot and we taught each other things that would help the other.

He was tasked with adding a plate to a truck so they could mount a compressor hose to air up tires while on recovery. Initially when we set things up, I signed on as the fire watch. That entailed getting everything that could be flammable out of the area so it would not catch on fire. So we set everything up, got everything together, and got it done. After we were done, he told me "I almost asked if you wanted to take a crack at doing the welding" I told him "I almost asked you if I could take a crack at it." He asked me "Why didn't you ask? I would have let you do it" I told him "I wasn't afraid you would say no, I was afraid you would say yes."

This is a perfect example of not feeling worthy of success. Let's face it: if I was on the way to screwing it up, he would have stopped me before things got too bad. He also knew I had a good head on my shoulders. I wasn't an idiot, and he knew I could do it. Also, I REALLY WANTED TO TAKE A CRACK AT IT! It boiled down to my fear of success, feeling of being unworthy. And while we were still friends, things were different after that.

A lack of self-esteem can do this to us as well. Thinking we are not worthy of success or even being given a chance can put a paralyzing fear of asking to do something or worse, refusing a chance that is given to us.

But I discovered that reclaiming self-esteem is a personal journey, one that demands recognition of our worth. We have to acknowledge that we are deserving of respect-respect that begins with ourselves.

Self-confidence and self-motivation serve as powerful tools for building self-esteem. When you embark on a task or pursue a goal with an unwavering belief that failure is not an option, your self-esteem soars! You radiate confidence and approach each day with a sense of empowerment.

Building self-esteem requires more than positive thinking; it necessitates deep internal transformation. Here are the key strategies to guide you on your path of self-discovery and empowerment:

1) Build assertiveness: Embrace the art of assertive communication. Learn to express your thoughts, emotions, and needs respectfully and confidently. By setting clear boundaries and standing up for yourself, you establish a solid foundation for self-esteem

2) Set realistic expectations: Rid yourself of the burden of perfectionism. Instead, focus on setting achievable goals and celebrating the progress you make along the way. Acknowledge that setbacks are a part of the journey, providing invaluable opportunities for growth.

3) Challenge negative beliefs: Dump the Head Trash! Get rid of the beliefs that have held you captive! Replace them with positive, empowering thoughts. Build self-acceptance and remind yourself of your strengths, past successes, and the progress you've achieved.

4) Foster a supportive environment: Surround yourself with people who uplift and support you. Seek out relationships and communities that foster positive self-esteem. Distance yourself from those who consistently undermine your self-worth or bring negativity into your life.

5) Practice self-care and self-compassion: Prioritize activities that build your physical, emotional, and mental well-being. Do self-care practices that bring you joy, relaxation, and renewal, kind of like

recharging your batteries. Welcome self-compassion, treating yourself with kindness, understanding, and forgiveness. This is the most important. We are the hardest on ourselves, therefore we need to be aware when we are beating ourselves up.

6) Remember your strengths and achievements. Recognize and celebrate your unique qualities, talents, and accomplishments. Honor your strengths and find opportunities to utilize them in your daily life. Doing activities that showcase your abilities will boost your self-esteem and bring a sense of fulfillment and pride.

7) Don't be afraid to ask for help with something. You do not have to walk this path alone. Reach out and ask trusted friends, family members, or even a coach or therapist when your esteem needs a boost. A therapist or a coach can provide a whole host of ideas and tools to help you get past underlying issues and boost your self-worth.

Reclaiming your self-esteem is a journey of self-discovery, self acceptance, and personal growth. Be patient with yourself, building esteem does take some time, but in the end it is worth it. As you start this journey, remember that your self-esteem is well within your power to reclaim.

With determination and the implementation of these strategies, you can break free from the chains of low self-esteem and step into a life where you fully recognize your worth, Welcome the journey, celebrate your progress, and believe in the potential that lies within you. You have the power to reclaim your self-esteem and create a life filled with confidence, joy, and fulfillment.

Chapter 6:
Summary of the First Parts:

Of the Program

In our quest for personal growth and self-improvement, we start on a journey. It begins with the recognition that we are capable of achieving greatness, and our actions and mindset shape our path.

We started our journey by understanding the importance of confidence. We learned that confidence is not just a trait possessed by a chosen few, but a skill that can be cultivated. By embracing positive self-talk, setting achievable goals, and developing resilience, we lay the foundation for a confident mindset that propels us forward.

Building on this foundation, we explored the power of positive thinking. Our thoughts have a profound influence on our attitudes, emotions, and outcomes. By cultivating gratitude, visualizing success, and reframing negative thoughts, we shift our perspective and invite more positivity in our lives. The magic of positive thinking lies in its ability to shape our reality and enhance our overall well-being.

But confidence and positive thinking alone are not enough.

We need self-motivation to turn our aspirations into actions. Self-motivation is the inner drive that fuels our pursuit of goals and propels us towards success. By understanding our personal motivations, setting meaningful and realistic goals, and breaking them down into manageable steps, we empower ourselves to take consistent action and make progress.

Yet, as we journey deeper into personal growth, we confront the obstacles of self-esteem. Our self-esteem is shaped by our experiences, the messages we receive from others, and our own beliefs about our worth. It can either empower us or hinder our progress. We realized the importance of cultivating self-esteem, which starts with recognizing our inherent worth and deserving respect. By embracing assertiveness, challenging negative beliefs, fostering a supportive environment, and practicing self-care and compassion, we embark on a path of self-discovery and empowerment.

These chapters form the cornerstone of our personal development program, laying the groundwork for a fulfilling and purposeful life. As we reflect on our journey so far, we see how confidence, motivation, and esteem work together to form our foundation of self-worth.

Our journey continues, and there is much more to explore and discover. But let's pause and celebrate the success we have had to this point. Each chapter has provided us with valuable insights and practical strategies. It is through understanding and applying these principles that we unlock our true potential and understand the power within us to forge our future, no matter what happened in our past.

As we turn the page to the next chapter, we carry with us the wisdom and lessons learned. We are ready to dive deeper into the confusing web of relationships-those connections that enrich our lives and shape our experiences. Together, we will navigate the complexities of human interactions and uncover the secrets to building meaningful and fulfilling relationships. After that we will explore the twists and turns of careers and how they can be great or detrimental to our well-being. This is why the first 3 parts are the most important: If these aren't in a good place, then everything else we attempt will be like a house of cards: doomed to failure no matter how hard we want it to work.

Chapter 7:
Relationships

Good relationships are no accident. They are the work of joy-
Dr. John Gottman

We've come a long way on our journey of self-improvement. We've built up our Self-Confidence, stoked our Self-Motivation, and nurtured our Self-Esteem. These three pillars form our rock solid foundation of our new life, and Self-Confidence stands out as the ultimate game changer in our new path.

Now that we walk with our heads held high, no longer hindered by thoughts of "I can't", but instead fueled by thoughts of "How Can I Get That Done?" It's time to shift our focus to the people in our lives. Are there any areas where we can improve our relationships and create more fulfilling connections?

In this chapter, we're diving headfirst into the delicate web of relationships. We're going to explore how our early experiences with our parents shaped our thought patterns and continue to influence us today. We'll unpack the truth about our spousal or significant other relationships and whether they truly align with our goals of a better life.

And let's not forget our buddies-the friends who've been there through thick and thin. Are they uplifting us, pushing us to grow, and celebrating our successes? Or are they unintentionally dragging us down with their negativity and holding us back from our true potential?

So, as we embark on this adventure, it's time to buckle up because this is going to be an exciting ride. Together we'll navigate the twists and turns of these relationships, shedding light on the challenges and discovering opportunities for growth and improvement.

PARENTAL

Let's take a moment to reflect on those early years and the lessons we learned through observing our parents. What did you observe in your youth? What do you remember both seeing and feeling about any particular situation? Was there a sense of waiting for good things to happen, a belief that good things would just fall into place? Or perhaps you grew up in a broken home, shuttling between each parent's house? Did bitterness from one parent or another seep into your young mind, witnessed from one parent or another?

Now, fast forward to your current relationship. Are there moments of bitterness between you and your partner? Or maybe you are living in perfect harmony. Maybe you have developed that mindset of waiting for something good to happen, with or without your active involvement. These thoughts and actions can often be traced back to the patterns we observed when we were young. It's worth taking a moment to really think about that, reflect and learn how those early memories and impressions are affecting us today.

Was there ever a time where you were disciplined for lying, but 10 minutes later you observed them lying to someone? That can be a mind scramble! Sitting there, wondering why there seems to be a double standard. You were told "You don't know how or when to do it" or "That's me, not you". I can relate, my friend, I've been there as well. I recall a time when my parents were separated, and my dad was talking to someone, blatantly saying something I knew wasn't true. I mustered up the courage to ask about it. The response? "It doesn't matter, we won't see that person again". Can you imagine the confusion and frustration that stirred within me? Why was it okay for him to bend the truth, but not for me? And the bigger question-why couldn't we just speak open and honestly about what was going on? As I write this, my anger is rising, not just from my own experiences but for every kid who has been in such a situation.

There was another incident I vividly remember. My dad was driving a truck, a car hauler, out of the Dallas area. They were distributing measuring sticks to check the height of the top of the cars, so they were within legal limits. Someone had already received theirs, but my dad was complaining about not getting his yet. I distinctly heard him say "I ought to go and take his stick out of his truck". Can you imagine the effect this has on a confused 14-year-old kid? What was I supposed to think? At the time, confusion consumed me. It didn't fully register at the time, but the impact lingered. How could such a thought process be even remotely acceptable, especially for a young teenager?

And then there was my mom. As I mentioned earlier, my parents split when I was ten, a couple of weeks before Thanksgiving. The emotions I felt when dad left were overwhelming-shock, confusion, and a sense of loss. My mom's health was already declining, and I believe there was already a victim mentality that contributed to my dad's departure.

No matter what was happening, my mom seemed to have a negative perspective on life. Happy thoughts were few and far between, and her mindset gradually declined as her health deteriorated.

These early experiences, the observations we made, and the emotions we absorbed from our parents can significantly shape our perceptions of relationships. It's essential to recognize how these experiences can significantly shape our perceptions of relationships. It's essential to recognize how these experiences may have influenced our current mindset and approach to love, connection, and communication.

So how do you get past these issues and others you might have acquired during your youth? Go back to the basics: Your Self-Confidence, Motivation, and Esteem play a huge part in getting past these issues and also a moral compass will help immensely. If it feels wrong, then don't do it or act on the thought. Whether your parents or parent did something, if it doesn't feel right to you, then don't do it.

<u>Friends and Acquaintances</u>

Are there people in your circles of friends who have either a negative thought process or just always have a negative comment to say no matter what is going on? There are many terms used to describe this, and I am going to use "Crab Mentality". If you have watched any episodes of Deadliest Catch on the Discovery Network, you have heard them describe how the crab mass works.

What happens when a crab starts to drift away from the mass, all the other crabs will reach up and pull it back into the mass. This is the same way some of our friends are. They have this negative outlook on life, and I'll tell you a secret: misery loves company and mediocrity loves company! What is happening here is people, whether subconsciously or not, will keep other people down to their level. If someone (you) are trying to improve their life, that will leave them behind, wallowing in their own mess, with no hope of getting themselves out. They are just like you were when you started this journey: trapped in their own prison while holding the keys to leave at their own will.

I have a friend, a friend of more than 2 decades, who has it in his head that he has to take a certain path in life. While I admire his dedication to it, I am also saddened by how he has wrecked his life in order to lose at this path. His credit is shot, his finances are in shambles, and he refuses to take a step back and reevaluate what is needed to succeed. He's about to take a trip and I'm afraid it is going to be devastating for him. Meanwhile he's trying to hold me back by involving me in his mess, and while I tell him on a regular basis there might be another way, he refuses to stop and think.

So I am having to distance myself from him and the

situation. While this hurts, it hurts more than I want to admit, it's something I have to do in order to keep my life and my business on track.

It's a sad thing. We became friends in college, and we always go to the range when we have a chance. This is going on a 26 year friendship, a friendship that might end, or at the very least, lessen in importance to maintain.

But these are the tough decisions that have to be made in order to improve our lives, to find our real purpose on this Earth. If the purpose outweighs the friendship, this is something that will have to be done.

Now is a good time to bring up loneliness. Everyone fears being lonely. I get it. But let's take a deep look into it and see if there is a benefit to it.

Have you ever had a computer slow down on you? You were working fine, then it started to slow down. Getting really sluggish. Having that frustration building while it kept slowing down.

What do you usually do? You shut down and restart the computer, right? Then what happens? It's working fine again! You are being productive, and all's right with the world. This is the same thing when it comes to loneliness. What you are doing is essentially rebooting your computer, the computer being your life. You are removing all the things that are slowing you down, making it sluggish to get anything done, and fixing any problems that were in your life and slowing you down from accomplishing anything.

To be fair, this won't happen as fast as restarting your computer. But it will be just as beneficial. So what do you do while you are "rebooting"? This is where you work on yourself.

This is where you maintain your self-confidence, motivation, and esteem you worked so hard on building before. Now you are thinking "I am alone". GOOD! Now think about all the time you were wasting on those who were dragging you down. Really think about it. Now think about all the time you now have to work on yourself and your goals. You probably have a good 3-4 hours every day to do those things now without the interference, and now is a good time to start.

SPOUSAL OR SIGNIFICANT Other Interference

This section is going to cause a lot of hate mail and fights. This is one area that is the most important. It also can be the most detrimental to your goal setting and accomplishments.

Imagine sitting in your car after a day's hard work. You can't stay there, but you don't want to go home. The reason is your spouse or significant other. You married indiscriminately or have a live in other, feeling pressured to marry and settle down while you can, and so you picked the lowest hanging fruit. Now you are a person of character. You made a promise to love and cherish until death do you part in the marriage, and in the significant other area you are making long term plans. But this gets difficult when you are coming home to about 10-15 boxes from Amazon guarding your front door every 2-3 days.

Now income isn't a problem, you are taking home over $83,000 per year, and your spouse or significant other doesn't have to work, while you are working 14-16 hours a day 6 days a week. You're tired. You're exhausted. All you want to do is get home and take a shower so you can relax a bit before going to bed. But there it is: The Barricade of Amazon blocking your entry into your house! There was a discussion about what was going on, and I was told all those things were on backorder when they were first ordered and they are just showing up. I didn't go looking into her Amazon account because I was respectful of her privacy and we had a budget agreement in place. But something was wrong.

There are also the dreams you've had, but when you bring them up, they are shot down worse than anything in TopGun: Maverick! Both of these instances have happened to me. I wanted to get back into broadcasting. We were at a Triple-A game and there was a local radio station I listened to on the way to work everyday doing a live remote. I started talking to the host, and since they were a new radio station, they were looking for on-air talent.

I COULD FEEL THE BURNING IN MY BACK! As I was talking to him, the (ex) wife was burning holes in my back! On the way home, she told me I was an idiot for even thinking about doing that. This is something I had always wanted to do, and even did it for a while after training. And I couldn't do it again? I couldn't even give it another try? What was she so against? Then the thought of "Aren't spouses supposed to be supportive?" came through my mind.

These and other thoughts kept racing around in my mind while she was berating me. All because I had a dream (actually a goal because there was a plan in place) and I wanted to pursue it.

This is where dread and resentment started to manifest itself. The resentment from the denial of attempting the goal, and the dread of going home because of the Guardians of Amazon were waiting for me at the house. I think also this was where I started referring to home as "the house" It didn't feel like a home, it was just a place to sleep. This should have been the first clue as to how bad things have gotten.

So, what happened? There was eventually a divorce, but it was too little, too late. There shouldn't have been any marriage to begin with, and it should have ended as soon as it began.

So what do you do to avoid this situation? First, don't get married 3 months after meeting someone. If you are in this situation, then there has to be a real hard talk about goals, dreams, and finances. And be prepared for a long talk. This will not go well unless both people in the relationship are ready to listen to the other and be open-minded. This does mean both of you. If you or the other is closed minded, this will not be a good talk.

Something else to think about is why you got married in the first place. For me, the pressure of being older (40) coupled with a previous failed marriage placed tremendous pressure on "getting it right" this time. This again is a wrong reason to get married.

This self-evaluation that you are doing needs to be done. You need to know if you married for the right reasons. This part doesn't require the spouse to be involved. This is a self-evaluation. Only after you do this will you know if you married for the right reasons. If you didn't, there are some tough choices to make, choices that your spouse might not like at all. But you have to do it for your benefit. This sounds selfish, but it is the hard truth if you want to have a happy and peaceful life.

<u>Co-workers</u>

There is a saying: you are married to your job. This has a grain of truth to it. You see your co-workers more than your family during the work week when you take out time for sleeping. You see your co-workers 40 hours a week in a normal job. Let's look at the time awake at home:

- Wake up at 6, morning wake up routine
- Leave for work at 7, figure an hour commute on average.
- Get there at 8, work until 5
- Leave work at 5, figure the hour commute back home
- Get home at 6. Family time until 10, then bed.

That's 4 hours a day with family, 5 days a week, for a total of 20 hours a week. And you can't even count the hour in the morning because you are getting ready for work. So in an average work week you are spending TWICE the time with your work family than your real family! Now you should ask yourself: Why are you dealing with negativity in the workplace?

- Her over there. Always taking credit for someone else's work

- Him in the next office. Doing the minimum to not get fired

- The Middle Manager. Trying too hard to improve himself, thus making everyone miserable.

- The person one floor below: No matter the situation, they always have a negative comment or attitude.

And you are spending TWICE the time with these people

in a work week than your own family! Is this any way to work or even exist? Of course it's not. But people do it everyday because they feel trapped in their job, or their career, and they are afraid of making a change.

As I have said before, it's because of the fear of the unknown. People fear what they don't know, thus trapping themselves in their situation and eventually taking on a form of Stockholm Syndrome, the identifying of their captors as a coping mechanism, out of a desire to survive. This is an extreme example, but it is appropriate to the point I am making.

I want you to ask yourself: Why are you dealing with this on a daily basis? Here's a hint: YOU ARE NOT A TREE! You are not planted there. You can move. All you have to do is look around a bit and see what is available. Right now there are more jobs than people willing to work, so finding some place else to work and doing the same thing you are doing now isn't going to be an issue.

It's your limiting beliefs and your fear of the unknown that is holding you back from just looking around. And I'll tell you why you aren't looking around: It's because you KNOW you can find something, it's just the fear of change that is keeping you right where you are! It's that line in the movie "Armageddon" all over again, where Billy Bob Thorton's character is stating "we have the ability to monitor about 3% of space." And we are afraid of the other 97% of what's out there. So here's a few tips you get yourself out of that situation:

- Have a talk with the person or people who are making it harder on everyone else. You don't know how things are going in their life, maybe there is something going on that they might want to talk about.

- Talk with like minded people who work with you. See if there is a way you can work together, keeping the negative and bad influencing people out of your new circle

- Limit time spent with the negative people who are dragging you and the rest of the workforce down. The less energy you spend on them, the more productive and better the mood you will have in general.

- If nothing else works or these options are not available, then a talk with HR might be in order. They might have other ideas or solutions that can help you get back to being the productive person you want to be. If that fails, then it's time to find somewhere else to work. You have to remember that your well-being is the most important in any endeavor you are undergoing. If that means finding another place to work, then that's something you have to do for yourself.

If the attitude of the company is indicative of the employees, then this is an indication of the total atmosphere of the company or branch as a whole. And that attitude comes from the top down-if the branch manager has this attitude, then all employees will eventually have this attitude.

This is also something to look at when interviewing for any job. Here's something to look for:

1) The company just hires "bodies", people to do the work and not really caring about how they are treated

2) The company is hanging on by a thread, and there is an air of panic in the atmosphere.

When a company just hires bodies to do work, they don't care about how their work environment is. All they will say is "make it better" or "this is how we do things". If either of those phrases are said, this is the time to keep them in mind, but keep looking. Remember, the right fit is out there, all it will take is a bit of looking around.

One particular company comes to mind. I was on a crew building retaining walls for a shopping district that was being built. All they were wanting was people to move the sand and concrete forms, not really wanting to teach much about anything. So when the project was finished they laid off all the recently hired people. And not one of us had any say in the matter. Now to be fair, this was during the summer in between semesters, but even back then I was picking up on this vibe, not understanding how to look for things like this. Because if you can pick up on this feeling, especially during an interview, then you will find a better suited job rather than wasting time with a job that won't appreciate you, and thus causing your esteem to start sliding down.

Another company, this was in the oilfield in West Texas, they were the worst company I worked for with regards to their attitude towards their employees. They made promises that were never kept, when (not if) they made mistakes on paychecks, they would immediately take out any overpayment, and if they shorted your paycheck, it took months before you would ever see the back pay, if they gave it at all. Even with a written agreement stating they wouldn't do that, they would constantly break their word, thinking you had nowhere else to go.

A lot of people who were leaving that company wanted me to go with them, knowing what I was capable of and how my work ethic is. But again, I made a commitment, so I stuck it out, to my eventual detriment. So the lesson here is: during the interview, I gathered they were in a constant hiring loop, just getting bodies to work the trucks and the derricks. I should have never gone past the first interview. But I did and I paid the price for it.

So catching these signs early on or leaving quickly, or not going to them at all, is the key to finding a great company, a company that values you and your thoughts.

Reflection and Action

As we reflect on the impact of our various relationships, it becomes clear that they play a significant role in our journey of self-improvement and personal growth. The influences of our parents and early experiences, the dynamics of our friendships, and the atmosphere in our workplace all shape our mindset, emotions, and aspirations.

But armed with self-confidence, self-motivation, and self-esteem, we have the power to transform our relationships and create a more fulfilling life. It begins with self-reflection and taking action to take better care of our emotional and physical self.

CHAPTER 8:

Careers

Choose a job you love and you will never work-
Mark Twain

I touched on this a bit (more of a rant, I know), but now that we have our core self worked out and we are building relationships both in our personal and professional life, now we can look at our career. Are we happy with where we work and in our line of work?

I get it. We have to work in order to pay bills. So we take the first job we can get so we can support ourselves and/or our families. But are we destined to stay in that job or career for the rest of our lives?

Absolutely not. Like I said in the previous chapter, we are not trees. We are not rooted, destined to stay in the same place forever. We can move. We can change our environment, and that does include our job or career if it is warranted.

So how does someone determine if they are in a good job with good people?

First, take a look around. Are there people who like and help one another in what they are doing? Does management or supervisors walk around seeing what they can do to help those under them?

Or do they talk badly about the company? Are people running to their cars, desperate to forget about the day and the job before they even get to their cars? Is there someone who likes to drink to forget where they work?

Or maybe it is a lack of satisfying work. The people are great, management is supportive, but you think you would be better suited in a different line of work. This is more common than you might think.

Good Work, Bad People

So what do you do in these situations? In the work area, when it comes to a negative work environment, you can talk to someone. You can ask (politely) if they could refrain from talking so negatively, and you would consider it a personal favor if they do so. Or if it is a middle manager, you can ask how you could help them achieve the goals that their supervisors have assigned them. Are they being pushed beyond what would be considered to be normal expectations? This happens a lot more than you would think. The pressure that a middle manager is feeling may not be coming from the workforce they are assigned to manage, but from the people above them. This one question has been known to show that you care, and thus cause the middle manager to feel better, then the whole mood of the department will be lighter.

There was a time where I had to deal with a middle manager who was trying real hard to push everyone. He was trying to get a promotion to a lower upper management position. He was being a real bear of a manager, always making comments about how things could be done more efficiently, not taking into account what else was going on or even what the thought process was of the situation.

We had a pretty good working relationship. Sometimes he would call me even if I was off just to get my point of view. I noticed that was happening less and less, so I pulled him off to the side and had a chat with him.

He told me that he was getting a lot of flack from the new general manager. Even though he didn't work for the company directly (the company was going through a buyout at the time), he was still dealing with this overbearing general manager who wanted to prove himself, show that he was in charge of everything and he didn't care what other people think.

I reminded him of how we used to operate. By finding out what needs to be done and getting it done with as little fanfare and talking to other people as little as possible. We did our thing, got it done, and went on with our lives, not caring if people figured out that we did it or not. The job got done, and that's all that mattered.

It was like a lightning bolt hit him in the face. Suddenly he got the smile back on his face, his stance was taller, and you could just see the confidence fill him up! It was magical.

So the next night, we went back to what we knew: getting things done in an efficient manner, quietly and quickly. And he and I both gave limited reports: just the facts and not much else in the way of details. And just like that, the pressure lessened, and he was back to his old self. He knew I would back his play, I would do what I could to help him, and I knew he had my back. You can probably guess this was one of those jobs that had both a negative atmosphere and negative people as supervisors.

But this is an example of how you can talk to someone and see if the pressure is from them or from somewhere else. You will find if the pressure is from somewhere else, then knowing you have their back will make them feel better, thus making the workplace a better place in general.

<u>Good People, Bad Job</u>

What about a job that you are good at, possibly an expert, but you are just going through the motions because you just don't like the work?

People come to you for just about everything because you are approachable, knowledgeable, and a good person in general. But you just don't like the work. You feel out of place, not really getting into a good rhythm and just waiting to clock out for the day. This is an indication of the job not being the right fit for you. And eventually you will burn out and all the work you did on self-improvement to this point will start to unravel and you will end up losing the job and having a negative reference on your resume. Is staying in a job that doesn't satisfy you and risking all of that worth it?

<u>Absolutely Not!</u>

So what do you do?

First, remember there are more jobs than people willing to work, so finding a different place to work is going to be easier. Second, this is a great time to figure out what your passion is. What do you want to do? Where are your interests?

A good rule of thumb is the quote at the beginning of this chapter. "Choose a job that you love, and you will never work" There have been many people that have used this quote, and I am referencing Mark Twain for it. But it is the truth. You have 168 hours in a week, and you have to work to pay bills and live a life, so you might as well do what you love.

Think about it. If you wake up every morning, looking forward to going to work, is it really working? You are going to be up anyway, so why not do something to occupy your time? And if you are going to be doing something, then why not do something you have a passion for? With this way of thinking, you will never work a day in your life.

Maybe working for someone or in a big company isn't for you. Maybe you have the entrepreneurial spirit within you and you might be better off working on your own business. This isn't a choice to be made lightly. There is a lot more to it than just doing the same thing as you would when you are working for someone else. There are a lot of other things to consider as well. Solo Entrepreneur or establish an LLC. Hire some of the work out or do it all yourself? These and other things need to be thought about and considered when you think about starting your own business.

These are all the possibilities that are open to you, and it's up to you as to what path and direction you want to take.

Chapter 9:
Wrapping It All Together

If we all did things we were capable of, we would truly astound ourselves.

Thomas Edison

The Journey of Self-Improvement

Throughout this transformative journey of self-improvement, we have explored the areas of self-confidence, self-motivation, self-esteem, relationships and careers. We have dug deep into the core of our being, discovering our hidden potentials and overcoming obstacles that hindered our progress. Now as we reach this pivotal point in our new path, let's take a moment to reflect on the wisdom we have gained and the path that lies ahead.

In Chapter 3, we started the journey of self-confidence and the importance it holds as the key that unlocks our true potential. We discovered that our beliefs shape our reality, and by building a positive mindset and embracing our strengths, we can overcome self-doubt and step boldly into the world.

Chapter 4 propelled us forward with the power of self-motivation. We learned that self-motivation is the driving force that propels us toward our goals. By aligning our aspirations with our passions and purpose, we harnessed the energy needed to persevere through challenges and achieve greatness.

With our self-confidence and self-motivation built up, we worked towards improving our self-esteem in Chapter 5. We realized that true self-worth comes from within, independent of outside validation. Through self-compassion, self-acceptance, and nurturing our strengths, we built a solid foundation of self-esteem, empowering us to embrace our uniqueness and radiate authenticity.

Chapter 6 was talking about how the first 3 areas of self improvement are the keys to moving forward to interactions with others. Without those first 3 steps in place, everything else will fall apart because we haven't set a good foundation within ourselves. This is why these steps are done in order. First, get the foundation set, then build up from there.

As we worked our way into the realm of relationships in Chapter 7, we uncovered intricate dynamics that shape our interactions with others. We acknowledged the influence of our early experiences with parents, recognizing how they impact our patterns of thinking and our approach to love, connection, and communication. We also looked at the importance of supportive friendships and how surrounding ourselves with positive influences will propel us to even better opportunities. Additionally we looked into the delicate balance of spousal and significant other relationships, recognizing the need for open communication, shared values, and mutual support and respect.

In Chapter 8, we learned about how careers are the cumulation of the process. When we have developed positive relationships both personal and professional, built on the foundation of self-confidence, motivation, and esteem, we find ourselves with more opportunities than we can keep track of.

We considered the reality that staying at a job or in a career that doesn't align with our passions and values can lead to burnout and dissatisfaction. We explored the negative signs of a negative work environment and offered strategies for working through challenging situations, whether through open communication or exploring alternate career paths. We encouraged the pursuit of work that ignites our passion and brings us joy, whether within a traditional job or entrepreneurial pursuits.

Now as we stand at this point in our journey, we are poised to embark on the next chapter in our lives. We have laid the groundwork for personal growth and meaningful connections. We have discovered the power within us to overcome obstacles and pursue a life of purpose and fulfillment. Armed with self-confidence, motivation, and esteem, we possess the tools to navigate the complexities of relationships and careers.

The road ahead may still be filled with challenges, but we have proven ourselves resilient and capable of growth. Let us carry the lessons we have learned, the insights we have gained, and the determination we have built into the future. Let's continue to embrace personal development as a lifelong journey, constantly evolving and striving for excellence.

As we turn the page to the next chapter of our lives, let us do so with a renewed sense of purpose and a steadfast commitment to living a life that aligns with our true selves. We are the authors of our destiny, and with each step we take, we shape the narrative of our own story.

FINAL THOUGHTS

As I sit in my backyard, contemplating the history that is my life, the lessons learned, and the ability to help others, I am overcome with emotion. When I first sat down to start note taking on this book, it occurred to me that I wouldn't get it all done the first time. I wouldn't get all the thoughts, the emotions, and the wisdom I have learned over a lifetime into this book. But

I realized that is okay. There is always another book, more people to help, and more wisdom to learn and give to others.

I hope this book helps you as much as the lessons I learned helped me.

Michael Barnes
Norman, Ok